COW TAILS & TRAILS

A Fun & Informative Collection of Everything Bovine

Published by
Willow Creek Press
P.O. Box 147
Minocqua, Wisconsin 54548

Editor/Design: Andrea K. Donner

Library of Congress Cataloging-in-Publication Data:

Cow tails & trails : a fun & informative collection of everything bovine.
       p. cm.
     ISBN 1-59543-156-X (hardcover : alk. paper)
     1. Cattle--Miscellanea. 2. Cattle--Pictorial works. 3. Cattle--United States--
Miscellanea. 4. Cattle--United States--Pictorial works. I. Title: Cow tails and
trails. II. Willow Creek Press
     SF197.4C69 2005
     636.2--dc22
                                                                    2005016324

Printed in Canada

Contents

The Cow's Story

When you watch a herd of Holsteins hanging
out in the pasture, slowly munching the grass,
chewing their cud, twitching their tails, and
sleeping contentedly on the ground, it's hard to imagine
they were ever "wild." And, of course, Holsteins never
were wild, but like all cattle, they are descended from one early
wild ancestor, the aurochs (*Bos primigenius*).

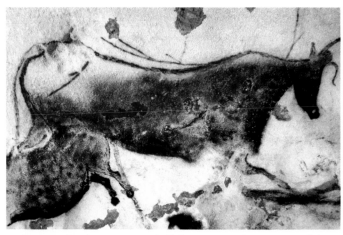

The aurochs, the ancestor of all domestic cattle, are one of the
animals painted on the famous cave walls near Lascaux, France.

The aurochs were huge animals that originated on the subcontinent of India and then spread into China, the Middle East, and eventually northern Africa and Europe. Aurochs are one of the animals painted on the famous cave walls near Lascaux, France. It is believed that the last surviving member of the species was killed by a poacher in 1627 on a hunting reserve near Warsaw, Poland.

Aurochs began to be domesticated by humans sometime between 8,000 and 10,000 years ago. Remains of domesticated cattle found in Turkey and other sites in the Near East have been dated to approximately 6,500 B.C., but the exact date of domestication is unknown. What is known is that cattle were domesticated after sheep, goats, pigs, and dogs. Eventually, two major types of aurochs developed: humped and humpless. The humpless cattle are the ancestors of today's Angus, Holstein, and other European breeds, while the humped cattle are the ancestors of Asian breeds, such as the Brahman.

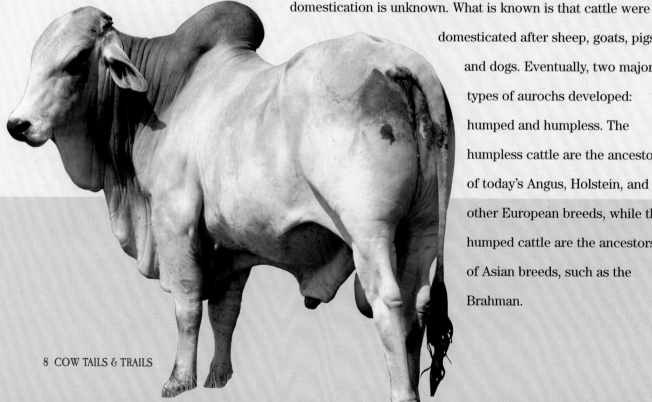

The American Bison is the only cattle species native to North America.
In the 1800s, people crossed the bison with domestic cattle and created the Cattalo,
a breed that was intended to give the domestic ox the bison's fur (and tolerance to cold).
In the long run, most attempts proved unsuccessful.

At first, cattle were mainly used for their strength. Sheep and goats were milked, while cattle were used to pull carts and to carry packs and people on their backs. Eventually, their draft purposes were largely replaced by horses, and much later by machinery, so cattle were selected more for single or dual purposes (milk and meat).

Devon cattle like these were the breed of choice for the Pilgrims, who used the adaptable animals for milk, draft, and beef.

In the 1920s, Dr. Lutz Heck, director of the Berlin Zoo, and his brother, Heinz Heck, each experimented separately with back-breeding cattle to try to create an animal that resembled the extinct aurochs. After twenty-five years of effort, the Heck brothers felt they had achieved the recreation of the aurochs, but geneticists are doubtful of their success. Today, approximately 150 descendants of the Heck brothers' cattle are still alive, and are known as Heck-ochs or Heck-Aurochs. Many can be seen by the public at zoos and game farms in western Europe.

© Leigh Rubin

Ayrshire

Brown Swiss

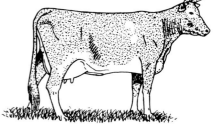

Guernsey

Angus

The development of the many modern breeds seen in North America today mainly took place in Europe. A "breed" is not a separate species, but simply a group of animals whose breeding habits have been manipulated by humans so that desired traits become more dominant. Whether using the animals for milk, meat, or both, the breeds we know in the United States today—Holstein, Guernsey, Jersey, Angus—were first developed in western Europe.

Holstein

Jersey

Purple

"Yes, ma'am, I can see that you're quite domesticated, but I was actually looking for *domestic* help."

© Leigh Rubin

Ever heard of a purple cow?

I never saw a purple cow,
I never hope to see one;
But I can tell you, anyhow,
I'd rather see than be one.

In 1896, humorist Gelett Burgess wrote this little four-line poem and published it in a San Francisco literary magazine called *The Lark*.

Coming to America

Domesticated cattle were brought to America in two ways: through Mexico in the sixteenth century, and from Europe with the first immigrant settlers. On the long voyage from western Europe, cattle provided milk and meat for the immigrants, and helped to settle the land once they arrived. The Devon breed was first brought to the Plymouth Colony in 1623, while the Holstein, Jersey, Angus, Guernsey, Shorthorn, and Hereford had all arrived by the end of the nineteenth century.

The Guernsey arrived in the United States in 1840.

The Ayrshire made it to America in the early 19th century.

The Texas Longhorn came into the United States through Mexico. The ancestors of the Longhorn were originally from Spain, and brought to the Caribbean by Christopher Columbus on his second voyage in 1493. Soon after, some of the animals were taken to Mexico and, by the middle of the sixteenth century, Longhorn cattle were brought into Texas and New Mexico where they thrived on the vast, open rangeland.

The Holstein arrived in 1852.

After the Civil War, there were over twenty-six million Texas Longhorn cattle roaming freely throughout the southwestern part of the United States. These are the cattle that were driven to market by the millions between 1866 and 1890. Today, however, Longhorn cattle are mainly kept for hobby rather than for commercial beef purposes.

COWBOYS & CATTLE DRIVES

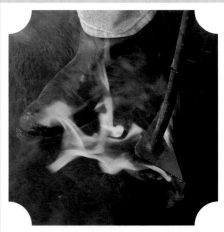

The life of the cowboys and their long cattle drives is a unique chapter of American history. By the mid-nineteenth century, the United States had acquired most of the western territories through treaties and acquisitions, and vast areas of grassland in the Texas, Oklahoma, and Wyoming territories were declared open range, where cattle were permitted to freely graze.

By 1860, twenty-six million cattle were counted in Texas, and because the cattle could wander over many miles of open range and mingle with the cattle of other ranchers, the system of branding cattle was started. Every spring, cowboys would gather up all of the cattle and every new young calf was branded with the owner's unique mark.

When the Civil War started in 1861, men from all over the country, including those in the western territories, flocked to join the Union or Confederate armies. During the course of the four-year war, western ranches were deprived of young men to handle the cowboy duties of branding and driving cattle to market. By the end of the war, great herds of unbranded cattle with no designated owners were populating the open ranges of the west.

Meanwhile, there was a great demand for beef on the eastern coast where supplies of cattle were severely depleted from the recently-ended Civil War. Texas cattle ranchers began hiring many cowboys to round-up and brand the unclaimed cattle and move them to the eastern markets.

Because the Texas rangelands were isolated from any easy transportation to the east, a cattle trail was established from northern Texas across Oklahoma to Abilene, Kansas, and the new railroad to the east. This route became known as the Chisolm Trail. Later, another route from west Texas to Denver, Colorado, became known as the Goodnight-Loving Trail.

Cattle dealers in Texas would hire a trail boss, a cook, several horse wranglers, and twenty to forty cowboys to drive a herd of several thousand cattle to market. The cattle had to be driven over 1,000 miles to the nearest railroad, and since cattle can move no more than ten miles per day without losing weight, an average cattle drive from Texas to Abilene, Wichita, or Dodge City, Kansas, lasted nearly four months.

The most cattle moved in one year was 700,000 head in 1871, and in total, between the years 1865 to 1895, ten million cattle

One pastime for the cowboys was to ride bucking steers during a roundup, an activity that has evolved into a large part of the modern rodeo.

were driven north from Texas. By the end of the nineteenth century, however, the railroads had penetrated most of the inaccessible parts of the southwest and long cattle drives were no longer necessary.

In the 1800s, cowboys really were cow "boys;" most of the young men were between fourteen and eighteen years old and their job was not an easy one. A cowboy's day started at sunrise and then, after a hearty breakfast, he would remain in the saddle for twelve or more hours, moving the herd further north. Nights were spent sleeping in the open around a campfire, or riding watch on the herd. When on watch, about four cowboys would slowly circle the herd to keep it contained and to guard against predators or rustlers. The sound of human voices, especially singing voices, would calm the cattle, so the cowboys on watch would usually sing as they rode.

...IN ADDITION TO INCREASED COSTS AND SHRINKING CORPORATE PROFITS, AS WELL AS THE POOR ECONOMIC CLIMATE, I'M AFRAID THE COMPANY HAS NO CHOICE BUT TO LET SOME OF YOU GO.

Thinning the herd

© Leigh Rubin

COWBOY SONGS FOR RIDING THE RANGE

Old Cowboys Lament

The range's filled up with farmers and there's fences ev'rywhere
A painted house 'most ev'ry quarter mile
They're raisin' blooded cattle and plantin' sorted seed
And puttin' on a painful lot o' style
There hain't no grass to speak of and the water holes are gone
The wire of the farmer holds 'em tight
There's little use to law 'em and little use to kick
And mighty sight less use there is to fight
There's them coughin' separaters and their dirty, dusty crews
And wagons runnin' over with the grain
With smoke a-driftin' upward and writin' on the air
A story that to me is mighty plain
The wolves have left the country and the long-horns are no more
And all the game worth shootin' at is gone
And it's time for me to foller, 'cause I'm only in the way
And I've got to be a-movin' – movin' on

Colorado Trail

Eyes like a morning star
Cheeks like a rose;
Laura was a pretty girl
God almighty knows;
Weep all you little rains,
Wail, winds, wail
All along, along along
The Colorado trail.
additional verses:
Ride, all the lonely night
Ride through the day,
Keep the herd a-movin' on
Movin' on its way.
Dark is the stormy night
Dark is the sky,
Wish I'd stayed in Abilene

Down in the Valley

Down in the valley, the valley so low
Hang your head over, hear the wind blow
Hear the wind blow, dear, hear the wind blow
Hang your head over, hear the wind blow

Writing this letter, containing three lines
Answer my question, will you be mine?
Will you be mine, dear, will you be mine?
Answer my question, will you be mine?

Write me a letter, send it by mail
Send it in care of the Birmingham jail,
Birmingham jail, dear, Birmingham jail
Send it in care of the Birmingham jail

Roses love sunshine, violets love dew
Angels in Heaven know I love you
Know I love you, dear, know I love you
Angels in Heaven Know I love you

Cattle Call

When the new day is dawning I wake up a yawning,
Drinking my coffee strong;
Make my bed in a role, down the trail I will stroll
Singing this old cattle call.

(yodel)

With my saddle all shedded and the cattle all bedded
Nothing wild seems to be wrong;
Make my bed 'neath the skies, I look up at the stars,
And then I can sing you this call.

Well, each day I do ride o'er a range far and wide.
I'm going home this fall;
Well I don't mind the weather, my hearts like a feather,

Back in the Saddle Again

I'm back in the saddle again, out where a friend is a friend,
Where the long horn cattle feed on the lonely jimson weed
I'm back in the saddle again.
Ridin' the range once more, totin' my old forty-four,
Where you sleep out every night and the only law is right,
Back in the saddle again.

Whoopi ti yi yo, rockin' to a fro, back in the saddle again
Whoopi ti yi   yea, I'll go my own way
Back in the saddle again.

Bury Me Not on the Lone Prairie

"O bury me not on the lone prairie"
These words came low and mournfully
From the pallid lips of the youth who lay
On his dying bed at the close of day.

"O bury me not on the lone prairie
Where the wild coyote will howl o'er me
Where the buffalo roams the prairie sea
O bury me not on the lone prairie"

"It makes no difference, so I've been told
Where the body lies when life grows cold
But grant, I pray, one wish to me
O bury me not on the lone prairie"

"I've often wished to be laid when I die
By the little church on the green hillside
By my father's grave, there let mine be
O bury me not on the lone prairie"

The cowboys gathered all around the bed
To hear the last word that their comrade said
O partners all, take a warning from me
Never leave your homes for the lone prairie"

"Don't listen to the enticing words
Of the men who own droves and herds
For if you do, you'll rue the day
That you left your homes for the lone prairie"

"O bury me not," but his voice failed there
But we paid no head to his dying prayer
In a narrow grave, just six by three
We buried him there on the lone prairie

We buried him there on the lone prairie
Where the buzzards fly and the wind blows free
Where rattlesnakes rattle, and the tumbleweeds
Blow across his grave on the lone prairie

And the cowboys now as they cross the plains
Have marked the spot where his bones are lain
Fling a handful of roses on his grave
And pray to the Lord that his soul is saved

In a narrow grave, just six by three
We buried him there on the lone prairie

Home On The Range

Oh give me a home, where the buffalo roam
And the deer and the antelope play
Where seldom is heard a discouraging word
And the skies are not cloudy all day.

(chorus)

Home, home on the range
Where the deer and the antelope play
Where seldom is heard a discouraging word
And the skies are not cloudy all day

How often at night, when the heavens are bright
With the light of the glimmering stars
I have stood there amazed, and asked as I gazed
If their glory exceeds that of ours.

The red man was pressed from this part of the west
He is likely no more to return
To the banks of Red River, where seldom if ever
His flickering campfires will burn.

I love the wild flowers in this bright land of ours,
I love the wild curlew's shrill scream;
The bluffs and white rocks, and antelope flocks
That graze on the mountains so green.

FARMING THROUGH THE TWENTIETH CENTURY

Farming practices have changed dramatically through the twentieth century. Primarily, the increased use of machines to perform work once done by humans or animals has raised farm efficiency while reducing the need for both human and animal labor. Additionally, farms have become much more specialized, with a smaller number of operators producing the majority of agricultural products consumed today.

Milk cans are a thing of the past in today's modern world.

#1

Texas is the big gun in the farming world. It leads the nation with the amount of land in farms with 130.5 million acres of farm and ranch land. It also leads the nation with the number of farms, with 229,000.

The total number of farms and land in farms in the United States is over 2,100,000 farms on over 938,000,000 acres.

The average farm size is 441 acres.

Leading states for farmland:
2. Montana (60.1 million acres)
3. Kansas (47.2 million acres)
4. Nebraska (45.9 million acres)
5. New Mexico (44.7 million acres)
6. South Dakota (43.8 million acres)
7. North Dakota (39.4 million acres)
8. Wyoming (34.4 million acres)
9. Oklahoma (33.7 million acres)
10. Iowa (31.7 million acres)

Leading states for numbers of farms per state:
2. Missouri (106,000 farms)
3. Iowa (90,000 farms)
4. Kentucky (87,000 farms)
5. Tennessee (87,000 farms)
6. Oklahoma (83,500 farms)
7. Minnesota (80,000 farms)
8. California (78,500 farms)
9. Ohio (77,600 farms)
10. Wisconsin (76,500 farms)

Guernsey dairy cows like these are partially responsible for the milk produced in the U.S., but the Holstein gets the credit for producing the most milk per cow.

The dairy industry has achieved significant production increases during the past century. The most cows were milked in 1944—an average 25.6 million head produced 117 billion pounds of milk. Since then, the number of cows has steadily dropped. Less than 20 million head were milked in 1957 and in 1990, the average number fell to less than ten million. At the same time, annual average production per cow has risen dramatically. In 1944, annual production per cow was 4,572 pounds. The average exceeded 5,000 pounds per cow for the first time in 1947, and 6,000 pounds per cow in 1956. The first 10,000 pound average was achieved in 1971, and 17,000 pounds per cow was reached at the end of the century. The country has definitely "Got milk"!

GOT MILK?

© Leigh Rubin

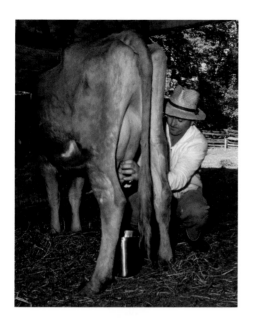

The number of milk cow operations has been declining in the U.S. for a number of years. There were 123,700 milk cow operations in the U.S. in 1997 compared to 97,560 in 2001. During this same period, the number of milk cows declined from 9.25 million head to 9.12 million head. Despite this decrease, however, the amount of milk obtained per cow keeps rising.

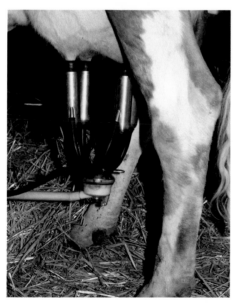

Milking cows by hand is definitely a thing of the past, and only seen today at historical exhibits (as shown in the top left photo) or on hobby farms. Single unit milking machines (bottom left) are now being replaced on large farms by automated milking machines (bottom right).

Who is the REAL dairy state?

VS.

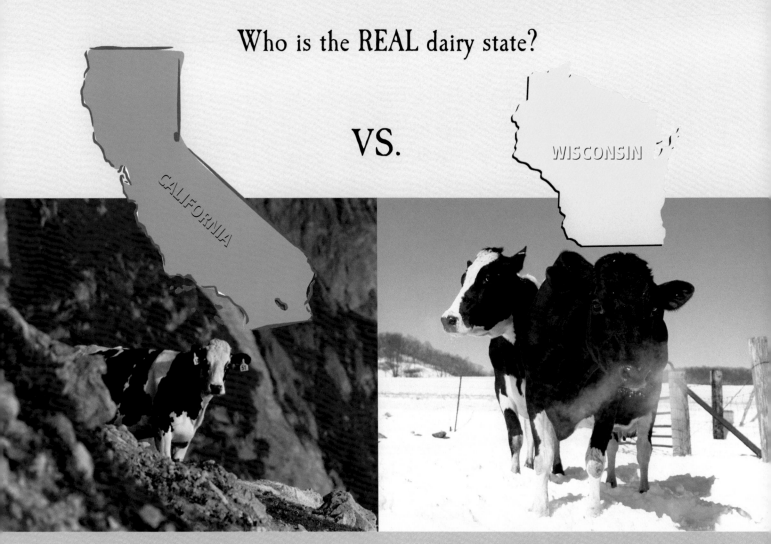

Dairy cows dotting California's rugged coastline are becoming an increasingly common sight.

Holsteins still brave the cold and produce millions of gallons of milk on Wisconsin's smaller farms.

Wisconsin and California are the top two states when it comes to dairy. Although Wisconsin has long been known as the dairy state, it has been edged out by California for the number one spot overall. Dairy accounts for only 14.5 percent of California's total farm receipts, however, while dairy is 48.3 percent of Wisconsin's total farm receipts. Wisconsin is also still full of Cheeseheads, as it makes the most cheese nationwide.

There are approximately 800,000 ranchers and cattlemen in the United States, raising cattle for beef in all fifty states. In 2003, cash receipts from livestock and livestock product marketing totaled over $98 billion—almost half of the total for all farm cash receipts in 2003 ($202 billion).

Total beef production in the United States during 2003 was 26.2 billion pounds (35.5 million head of cattle). Cattle averaged about 1,230 pounds before harvest, with an average carcass weight of 746 pounds (which translates into about 522 pounds of beef).

There are approximately 96 million cattle in the United States, made up of the following animals:

33,000,000 beef cows   9,000,000 milk cows

20,000,000 heifers   16,500,000 steers

2,200,000 bulls   15,400,000 calves

Hereford cow and calf

PARTS OF A COW

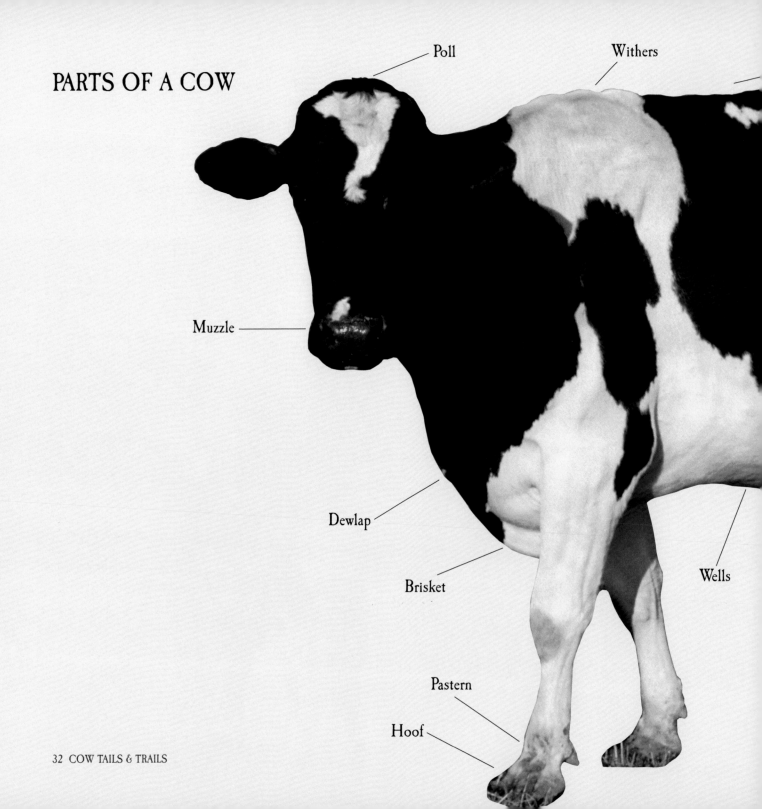

Poll

Withers

Muzzle

Dewlap

Brisket

Wells

Pastern

Hoof

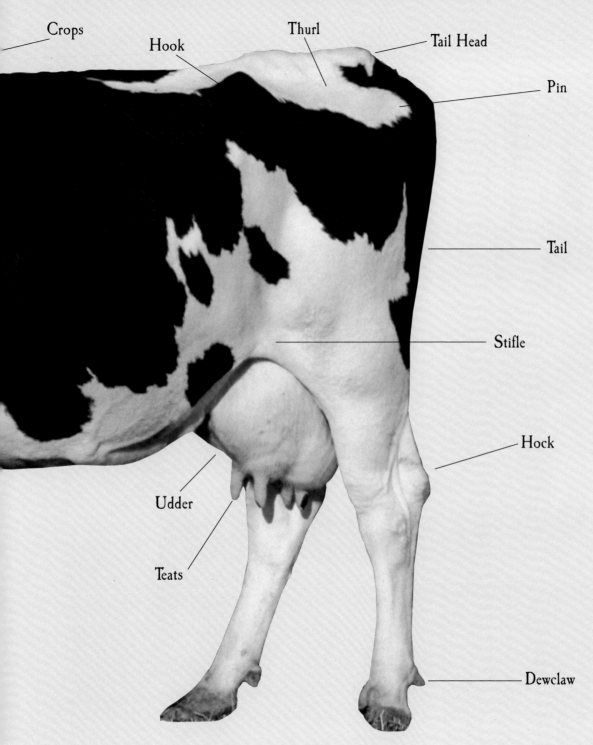

Crops

Hook

Thurl

Tail Head

Pin

Tail

Stifle

Hock

Udder

Teats

Dewclaw

COMMON COW TERMS:

A BULL is a mature male who has not been castrated.

A COW is a mature female with at least one calf. A cow's age is based on her age when she first has a calf.

A STEER is a young ox who has been castrated before reaching sexual maturity. Steers are usually raised for beef

A HEIFER is a young female cow that has not yet had her first calf. Most heifers have their first calf when are are about two years old, depending on the breed.

An OX is an adult castrated male.

LESS COMMON COW TERMS:

A DOGIE is a motherless calf.

A WEANLING is a weaned calf.

A YEARLING is a calf that is twelve to eighteen months of age.

A LONG YEARLING is an animals between nineteen months and two years of age.

A BULLOCK is a young bull, typically less than 20 months of age.

A FREEMARTIN is a female calf of a set of twins where the other calf is a male. Most of these animals are infertile.

SPRINGERS are jumping calves in the springtime.

A GOMER is an out-of-control animal.

A FEEDER CALF is one that will gain weight if placed on feed; they are raised specifically for beef.

A MULEY is a hornless cow.

STOCKER CATTLE are what feeder calves are called after they have been weaned and are less than 800 pounds.

A HARD KEEPER is a feeder that grows or fattens slowly on any type of feed.

A MAVERICK is a cow that has escaped being branded.

A SUCKLER is a cow that is giving milk to a calf.

"My gawd, Herb, just because you have four stomachs doesn't mean you have to stuff each and every one of them!"

Cattle are ruminants, which means they are even-toed hoofed mammals that chew cud and have a complex, usually four-chambered stomach.

Contrary to popular belief, cows do not have four stomachs; they have four digestive compartments. The four parts of the stomach are called the rumen, the reticulum, the omasum (or "manyplies"), and the abomasum. The rumen (or paunch) is where food goes when the cow swallows the first time. It holds over thirty gallons of partially digested food that is then regurgitated to be chewed as cud. When the cud is swallowed a second time, it goes directly to the second chamber, the reticulum (also called honeycomb), and then on to the omasum, which acts as a sort of filter. Then the food finally reaches the abomasum, the only chamber that acts as a true stomach.

A cow chews its cud for about eight hours each day (more time than it spends eating the food in the first place).

Cattle are also identified by having hollow, curved horns that stand out laterally from the skull. Those cows that don't have horns, either because they've been removed or because the breed has been designed so they don't grow anymore, are called "polled."

Most dairy breeds in the United States are born with horns but they are polled soon after they are born.

Polled heifers

Artificial insemination has had a tremendous impact on genetic improvement of almost all of the breeds. The semen freezing process was perfected in the late 1940s, and artificial insemination has allowed the use of superior, proven bulls by cattle breeders around the world. For example, artificial insemination accounts for 85 percent of Holstein births today, and it allows a single Holstein bull to sire as many as 50,000 daughters.

MANURE AND METHANE

A mature beef cow can produced about 75 pounds of manure per day (about nine gallons per day). A mature dairy cow can produce 115 pounds of manure per day (about fourteen gallons per day). What do farmers do with all this manure? Manure is most often used as a fertilizer for land application. Nutrients found in the manure include nitrogen, phosphorus, and potassium, but the manure must be applied carefully because too many nutrients can harm crop growth, contaminate the soil, and cause surface and groundwater pollution.

Large farm operations often use an effective *anaerobic digester* to process their manure (basically, bacteria breaks down the manure and produces usable methane). Manure mixtures that are treated anaerobically produce biogas and a stable liquid. Biogas contains about forty to sixty percent methane and can be used to run an engine generator to produce electricity, or it can be burned for heat. The disadvantages to this system are that it is very expensive, so its use is limited to very large livestock operations, the gas has a relatively low BTU output, and the gas is corrosive to generator engines. Research is in progress to make the process more practical for energy production.

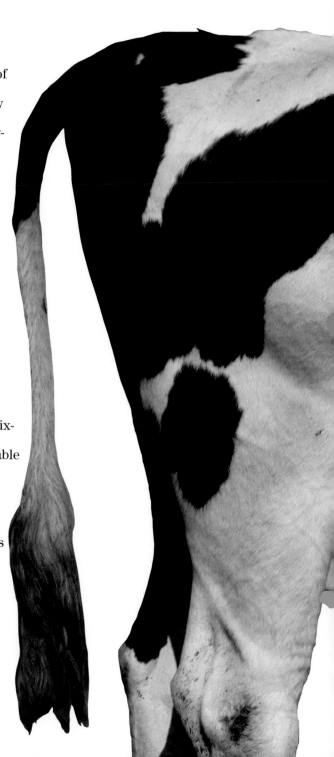

The Breeds

There are over nine hundred different
breeds of domestic cattle found throughout
the world, and they come in a wide variety of
shapes, sizes, and colors. In the United States, cattle
are used almost exclusively for dairy or meat purposes,
as draft animals are no longer necessary. Six main dairy breeds and
multiple beef breeds make up most of the cattle herds in the U.S.

The unique-looking Dutch Belted breed
also has a unique, all-black tongue.

The six main dairy breeds milked in the United States today, in order of popularity, are the Holstein, Jersey, Brown Swiss, Guernsey, Ayrshire, and the Milking Shorthorn. Out of these breeds, however, it is the Holstein that makes up ninety-five percent of all the cows milked in the U.S.

Nine out of every ten dairy farmers milk the incredible, milk-making Holstein!

The black-and-white Holstein is also the ubiquitous animal that most people think of when they hear the word "cow," and it is this cow's unique markings that decorate coffee mugs, curtains, salt and pepper shakers, shower curtains, and other cow-themed products. The Holstein is also the most productive milk maker of all the dairy breeds. On average, one Holstein cow produces over 17,000 pounds of milk and 630 pounds of butterfat per year.

The Holstein originated in the Netherlands, specifically in the two northern provinces of North Holland and Friesland. The original stock were the black animals and the white animals brought to the area by the Batavian and Friesian tribes about 2,000 years ago. The Holstein was strictly bred to produce efficient, high-producing animals that performed well on the area's grasslands. By 1865, these exceptional dairy cows were known as "Holland" or "Dutch" cattle. They were re-named Holstein-Friesian, which was later shortened to Holstein.

Holsteins are usually black-and-white, although red-and-white is sometimes seen, as are all-white and all-black animals.

Supersoaker fights on the dairy farm.

The Holstein was first brought to America by a Dutch sailing master who landed at Boston in 1852. The cow had supplied fresh milk for the crew during the voyage. Once in Boston, the cow was sold to Winthrop Chenery, a Massachusetts breeder, who was so impressed with the breed that he made additional importations in subsequent years. Soon other breeders were also establishing Holsteins in America. After about 8,800 Holsteins were imported, cattle disease broke out in Europe and importation ceased. Today, Holsteins are found on every continent and in almost every country in the world.

Holstein Facts

- Bulls weigh approx. 2,200 pounds and stand 5½ feet tall.

- Cows weigh approx. 1,500 pounds and stand 4½ feet tall.

- Calves weigh about 90 pounds or more at birth.

- Holstein heifers can be bred at 15 months of age, but most don't have their first calf until they are between 24 and 27 months old.

The Holstein's incredible milk yields are achieved partly through genetics and partly through modern technology: they are fed concentrated feed, receive attentive veterinary care, and are housed and milked in environmentally-controlled barns.

ENGLISH CHANNEL

Isle of Jersey

The Jersey is one of the oldest dairy breeds, having been recorded as purebred for nearly six centuries. It originated on the small Island of Jersey, one of the Channel Islands located on the French side of the English Channel in sight of the Normandy Coast. Because the island is so small (only seventy square miles), with limited pasture land, the cows are tethered on a short chain to graze in a small circle, and then moved several times a day to make maximum use of available grass.

Jerseys were known in England as early as 1771 and were regarded very favorably because of their milk and butterfat production. At that early date, the cattle of Jersey Island were commonly referred to as Alderney cattle, although that name is now obsolete. Similar to Holsteins and Guernseys, Jerseys were first brought to the United States in the 1850s on sailing vessels.

Jersey Facts
• Bulls weigh approx. 1,500 pounds and stand 4 feet tall.
• Cows weigh approx. 1,000 pounds and stand 3¾ feet tall.

Jerseys are adaptable to a wide range of climactic and geographic conditions, and they are found from Denmark to Australia and New Zealand, from Canada to South America, and from South Africa to Japan. They are excellent grazers and perform well in intensive grazing programs.

Jerseys are known for being cute! With their small stature, fawn coloring, and doe-like eyes, their refined appearance has made them a favorite decorative as well as productive animal. Victorian gentlemen farmers particularly liked the breed for this reason.

Jerseys produce the richest milk in percentage of butterfat and protein, and they are more tolerant of heat than the larger breeds. With an average weight of 900 pounds, the Jersey produces more pounds of milk per pound of body weight than any other breed. Most Jerseys produce far in excess of thirteen times their bodyweight in milk each lactation.

The Brown Swiss is, obviously, from Switzerland! The area of Schwyz was the scene of most of the early improvement, and in Switzerland the breed is often referred to as Schwyzer or Brown Schwyzer. It is also known as Braunvieh in German speaking countries.

The Brown Swiss is believed to be one of the oldest dairy breeds in the world. The cow only became known outside of Switzerland in the mid-nineteenth century when its meat became popular in France and Italy.

The Brown Swiss is a large, docile breed that is valued for its strength and ruggedness. Switzerland is a very rough and mountainous country that is covered with rocks, lakes, rivers, snow-capped mountains and glaciers. In the summer, many of the dairy herds are taken into the mountainous regions and are grazed on the abundant pastures and meadows that result from the heavy rainfall. As fall approaches, the cattle are returned to the lower lands where they are stabled or housed for the winter.

The Brown Swiss (above) resembles the Jersey in coloration, but the larger Brown Swiss has a fuller body shape and a more rugged appearance. The Jersey (below) is noted for its angularity, as seen in the protruding hips.

The Brown Swiss' color can vary from light to dark brown. The muzzle is banded, like the Jersey's, and it has large, fuzzy ears.

Brown Swiss Facts

• Bulls weigh approx. 2,000 pounds and stand 4¾ feet tall.

• Cows weigh approx. 1,400 pounds and stand 4¼ feet tall.

The Brown Swiss first came to America in 1869.

The small, brown-and-white Guernsey produces the rich and delicious golden Guernsey milk. The breed was started by a group of monks on the Isle of Guernsey, a small island in the English Channel off the coast of France, over a thousand years ago. The monks brought to the island the best bloodlines of French cattle—Norman Brindles, also known as Alderneys (now extinct), and the famous Froment du Leon breed from Brittany—and developed the Guernsey. Over the centuries, Guernseys remained in relative isolation and in the nineteenth century, the government passed a law prohibiting the import of other cattle to keep the breed pure.

The Guernsey made it to America in the fall of 1840 when three Alderney cows were brought to New York. Soon after, two heifers and a bull were also imported from the Island. In 1868, American farmers began importing the cows in larger numbers, and in 1877, the American Guernsey Cattle Club (now the American Guernsey Association) was founded to preserve the purity of the breed.

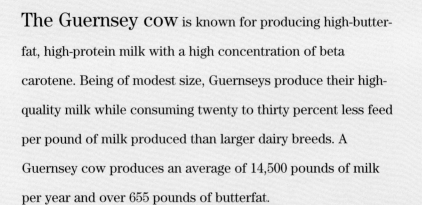

The Guernsey cow is known for producing high-butter-fat, high-protein milk with a high concentration of beta carotene. Being of modest size, Guernseys produce their high-quality milk while consuming twenty to thirty percent less feed per pound of milk produced than larger dairy breeds. A Guernsey cow produces an average of 14,500 pounds of milk per year and over 655 pounds of butterfat.

Guernsey Facts

• Bulls weigh approx. 1,700 pounds and stand 4¼ feet tall.

• Cows weigh approx. 1,100 pounds and stand 4 feet tall.

• Guernseys have a younger average age of first calf heifers than the larger breeds.

The Ayrshire originated in the highlands of County Ary, Scotland, where the farmers needed a dairy cow that could withstand the rugged highland weather. During its development, it was first called the Dunlop, then the Cunningham, and finally the Ayrshire. The principal ancestor of the breed was the Teeswater, which later was largely used in the formation of the Shorthorn breed in England.

An efficient grazer, the Ayrshire was well suited for the land and climate in Ayr. The breed was imported into the United States in the early nineteenth century by new England dairy farmers who needed cows that could graze on their rough, rocky farmland and who could tolerate the cold winters. Because the New England environment was very similar to the cow's native Scotland, the breed thrived in the new world.

Ayrshire Facts

- Bulls weigh approx. 1,850 pounds and stand 4½ feet tall.
- Cows weigh approx. 1,200 pounds and stand 4¼ feet tall

The Ayrshire cow is considered to be one of the most beautiful of the dairy cattle breeds. The reddish-brown mahogany spots are usually very jagged at the edges and often small and scattered over the entire body of the cow. The color markings can vary from nearly all red to nearly all white, and in some animals, especially the bulls, the reddish color can be so dark as to appear almost black against the white background.

The Ayrshire's horns were a hallmark of the breed for many years. These horns often reached a foot or more in length and, when properly trained, gracefully curved out, up, and slightly back. When polished for the show ring, the Ayrshire horns were a beautiful sight. Unfortunately, the horns were not practical, and today almost all Ayrshires are de-horned (polled) as calves.

The Milking Shorthorn, as part of the Shorthorn breed, is one of the oldest recognized breeds in the world. They originated in northeastern England in the Valley of the Tees River. Shorthorns first came to the United States in 1783, when "milk breed" Shorthorns came to Virginia. These early importations, often called "Durhams," continued during the early 1800s, and the first herd west of the Mississippi River was established in 1839. Because of its hardiness, adaptability to changing environments, and efficiency of production, the Milking Shorthorn was the breed of choice for the pioneers, furnishing them with meat, milk, and power as they moved west.

ENGLAND

The Milking Shorthorn is the most versatile of all the

breeds, which is one of its greatest attributes. They adapt well

to both hot and cold climates, and it is the only breed in the

United States today considered to be a dual-purpose breed.

Along with the Friesian, the Shorthorn has had the most wide-

spread and pervasive influence on the world cattle population.

Other dairy breeds milked in the United States include the Kerry, the Canadienne, the Dutch Belted, the Milking Devon, and the Norwegian Red. The Dutch Belted, below, is one of the most unique looking cows. It was bred by Dutch noblemen who wanted their cows to have a noticeably different look. The breed flourished in the United States as a dairy breed from around 1815 to 1940.

Any of the breeds can be crossed with other breeds to make some interesting looking new bovines. The cow above is a cross between a Holstein and a Dutch Belted, while the cow to the right is a cross between a Holstein and an Angus. Crossbreeding is more common in beef cattle than in dairy cattle.

There are numerous beef breeds found throughout the United States, but the most common are the Angus, Hereford, and Shorthorn. Other noted breeds are the Charolais, Limousin, Simmental, Pinzgauer, Devon, Highland, and Brahman. Many cattle raised for beef are crosses of these breeds. The popular Black Baldie, shown below, is not considered a separate breed, but is a cross between the white-faced Hereford and the all-black Angus.

The Brangus is a cross between a Brahman and an Angus (it must be three-eighths Brahman and five-eighths Angus), and is considered by many beef producers to be the most trouble-free cow in the industry because it adapts so well to any climate.

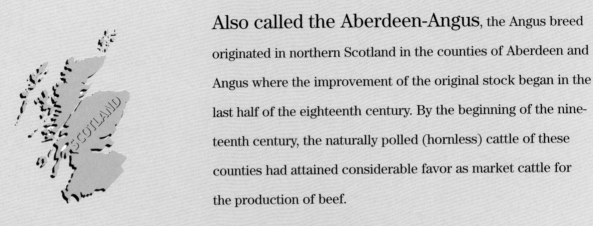

Also called the Aberdeen-Angus, the Angus breed originated in northern Scotland in the counties of Aberdeen and Angus where the improvement of the original stock began in the last half of the eighteenth century. By the beginning of the nineteenth century, the naturally polled (hornless) cattle of these counties had attained considerable favor as market cattle for the production of beef.

Four Angus bulls were brought to Kansas from Scotland in 1873, and when they were shown at a livestock exhibition, some people thought they were odd because of their polled heads and solid black color. Their hardiness and early maturity, however, quickly made them popular and more animals were imported directly from Scotland. Between 1878 and 1883, more than 1200 Angus cattle were brought to America, mainly to the midwest.

"Ironic, isn't it? ... Apparently we're good enough to serve but not good enough to be served."

© Leigh Rubin

Bred exclusively for their beef from the very beginning, the solid-black Angus is known for having the finest quality beef of the industrial breeds. Angus beef consistently ranks first in taste, texture, and color, and is the only beef marketed as a "name brand" meat.

Angus Facts

- Bulls weigh approx. 2,000 pounds and stand 4½ feet tall.
- Cows weigh approx. 1,150 pounds and stand 4 feet tall.

ENGLAND

The Hereford breed originated in Hereford County, England in the eighteenth century when breeder Benjamin Tomkins first developed the fast growing, hardy yet docile, high-quality beef cattle. This original, multiple-purpose Hereford was entirely red in color; it wasn't until the early nineteenth century that another breeder, John Hewer, introduced the familiar white face seen on Herefords today.

Herefords arrived in America in the nineteenth century where they became extremely popular, especially towards the end of the century when western expansion was at its height. Herefords were regularly bred with longhorns to improve the longhorn's meat quality. For this reason, Hereford's became known as "the great improver" of western cattle.

The Hereford is one of the most popular beef breeds in America.

There are two kinds of Herefords today, horned and polled. The Polled Hereford (simply the Hereford without its horns) was developed in the late 1890s by midwestern breeders who wanted the breed's outstanding beef-producing characteristics, but with the added desirable trait of being naturally hornless. Polled Herefords are one of the few breeds that began in the United States and were exported to England in the 1950s.

"There's no point losing sleep worrying about the bills—we'll just auction off the kids."

© Leigh Rubin

Hereford Facts

• Bulls weigh approx. 2,200 pounds and stand 4½ feet tall.

• Cows weigh approx. 1,500 pounds and stand 4¼ feet tall.

FRANCE

The large, white to creamy-white Charolais originated in central France in the provinces of Charolles and Nievre where they were known early on for their high-quality beef. The French bred these cattle for size and brawn, along with rapid growth and a large overall size. Although they were originally used for draft, milk, and meat, the Charolais was primarily selected for its beef traits.

In the 1920s, Charolais were first brought to Mexico from France, and then later, in the 1930s, they were brought into the United States from Mexico. Importation was stopped in the mid-1940s because of an outbreak of Hoof and Mouth Disease in Mexico, but in 1965, Canada lightened its import restrictions and again allowed purebred Charolais to be imported directly from France.

The Shorthorn is descended from Teeswater cattle, the large cattle that inhabited the valley of the Tees River on the northeast coast of England in the counties of Northumberland, Durham, York, and Lincoln. Also once called Durham cattle, the breed became popular in the 1700s and was brought to America in the late 1800s.

The Shorthorn is one of the most versatile of breeds and has historically been used for both beef and milking. Today in the United States, the two lines are separated into beef and milking, with the beef line the more popular of the two. The shorthorn is known for being hardy and easy to manage. If not polled, then the breed does have short horns, which curve slightly with age.

The Limousin breed, native to the south central part of France in the regions of Limousin and Marche, has always been bred for beef, and was introduced to the American beef industry in the 1960s. Originally from a rough, rocky area with a harsh climate, these cattle are extremely sturdy and adaptable. The Limousin has been nicknamed the "carcass breed" because of its exceptional beef traits.

Simmental means "Simme Valley" in German, which is the area of Switzerland where this breed was first raised and developed. The Simmental is one of the oldest and most widely-distributed breeds in the world, having spread to all six continents with an estimated forty to sixty million Simmental cattle world-wide (the Swiss cow population is fifty percent Simmental). The breed is used for both beef and dairy, but American farmers primarily use only the beef line.

The Brahman breed is the "sacred cattle of India" and those of the Hindu faith will not eat meat from them, will not permit them to be slaughtered, and will not sell them. The Brahman originated for *Bos indicus*, the humped line of the *Bos* species. They are intelligent, hardy, and very tolerant of hot, humid weather. For this reason, Brahman are most often seen in the southern part of the United States.

The brown-and-white Pinzgauer gets its name from the Pinzgau district in the province of Salzburg, Austria, where the breed was documented as early as the 1600s. This medium-sized cow has historically been used for both meat and milk. By 1990, there were over 30,000 Fullblood and Purebred Pinzgauers in the United States.

A rare breed in the United States, the tiny but tough Dexter is one of the smallest breeds in the world. They originated in the southern part of Ireland and are believed to be a cross of the Kerry and some other breed. Used for both dairy and beef, the Dexter is often called the ideal family cow because of its small size (mature bulls weigh less than 1,000 pounds and measure 38 to 44 inches at the shoulder, while cows weigh less than 750 pounds and measure 36 to 42 inches.)

Because the Longhorn has been on American soil for almost 500 years, and for most of that time it has lived "wild," it is a breed that has adapted well to the rough ranges of the southwestern United States. Today, cattle producers are looking to the Texas Longhorn for unique genetic material that will make other breeds more hardy, adaptable, and disease resistant, with the ability to browse marginal rangelands more efficiently.

CATTLE BREEDS OF THE WORLD

Africander
Albères
Alentejana
Allmogekor
American
American White Park
Amerifax
Amrit Mahal
Anatolian Black
Andalusian Black
Andalusian Grey

Angeln
Angus
Ankole
Ankole-Watusi
Argentine Criollo
Asturian Mountain
Asturian Valley
Aubrac
Aulie-Ata
Australian Braford
Australian Friesian Sahiwal

Australian Lowline
Australian Milking Zebu
Ayrshire
Bachaur
Baladi
Baltana Romaneasca
Barka
Barzona
Bazadais
Béarnais
Beefalo
Beefmaker
Beefmaster
Belarus Red
Belgian Blue
Belgian Red
Belmont Adaptaur
Belmont Red
Belted Galloway
Bengali
Berrendas
Bhagnari
Blacksided Trondheim and
    Norland
Blanca Cacereña
Blanco Orejinegro

Blonde d'Aquitaine
Bonsmara
Boran
Bordelais
Braford
Brahman
Brahmousin
Brangus
Braunvieh
British White
Brown Swiss
Busa
Cachena
Canadienne
Canary Island
Canchim
Carinthian Blond
Caucasian
Channi
Charbray
Charolais
Chianina
Chinampo
Chinese Black-and-White
Cholistani
Corriente

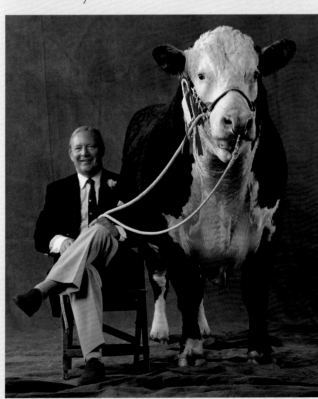

Prize-winning Hereford bull

Costeño con Cuernos

Dajal

Damascus

Damietta

Dangi

Danish Jersey

Danish Red

Deoni

Devon

Dexter

Dhanni

Dølafe

Droughtmaster

Dulong

Dutch Belted

Dutch Friesian

East Anatolian Red

Enderby Island

English Longhorn

Estonian Red

Evolène

Fighting Bull

Fjall

Finnish

Florida

Cracker/Pineywoods

Galician Blond

Galloway

Gaolao

Gascon

Gelbray

Gelbvieh

German Angus

German Red Pied

Gir

Glan

Gloucester

Greek Shorthorn

Greek Steppe

Groningen Whiteheaded

Guernsey

Guzerat

Hallikar

Hariana

Hartón

Hays Converter

Hereford

Herens

Highland

Hinterwald

Holando-Argentino

Holstein

Horro

Hungarian Grey

Icelandic

Illawarra

Indo-Brazilian

Irish Moiled

Israeli Holstein

Israeli Red

Istoben

Jamaica Black

The famous Normande breed from northern France is called the "Queen of Camembert" for the well-known French cheese.

Jamaica Hope

Jamaica Red

Jaulan

Jersey

Kangayam

Kankrej

Karan Fries

Karan Swiss

Kazakh

Kenwariya

Kerry

Kherigar'

Khilla'

Kho

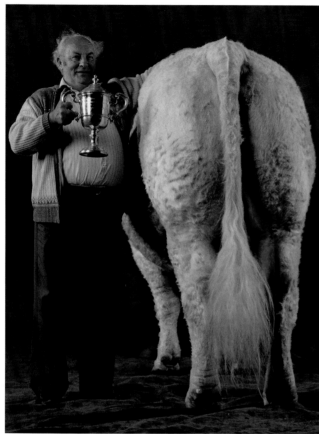

This champion Charolais is named Une de Mai. The Charolais breed is France's leading beef cattle.

Opposite page: Pimpernel Simmental bull

Kilis	Limpurger	Madagascar Zebu	Oropa
Krishna Valley	Lincoln Red	Maine Anjou	Ovambo
Kurdi	Lithuanian Red	Malvi	Parthenais
uri	Lohani	Mandalong	Philippine Native
vian Brown	Lourdais	Marchigiana	Polish Red
ousin	Luing	Maremmana	Polled Hereford
		Masai	Ponwar
		Mashona	Piedmontese
		Maure	Pinzgauer
		Mazandarani	Qinchuan
		Meuse-Rhine-Yssel	Rätien Gray
		Mewati	Rath
		Milking Devon	Rathi
		Milking Shorthorn	Red Angus
		Mirandesa	Red Brangus
		Modicana	Red Pied Friesian
		Mongolian	Red Poll
		Montbéliard	Red Polled Østland
		Morucha	Red Sindhi
		Murboden	Red Steppe
		Murray Grey	Reggiana
		Nagori	Retinta
		Nanyang	Rojhan
		N'dama	Romagnola
		Nelore	Romosinuano
		Nguni	Russian Black Pied
		Nimari	RX3
		Normande	Sahiwal
		Norwegian Red	Salers
		Ongole	Salorn
		Orma Boran	Sanhe

Santa Cruz	Simmental	Texas Longhorn	Ural Black Pied
Santa Gertrudis	Siri	Texon	Vestland Fjord
San Martinero	Slovenian Cika	Tharparkar	Vestland Red Polled
Sarabi	South Devon	Tswana	Vosges
Senepol	Sussex	Tuli	Wagyu
Sharabi	Swedish Friesian	Turkish Grey Steppe	Welsh Black
Shetland	Swedish Red-and-White	Ukrainian Beef	White Cáceres
Shorthorn	Swedish Red Polled	Ukrainian Grey	White Park
Siboney	Tarentaise	Ukrainian Whitehead	Xinjiang Brown
Simbrah	Telemark	Umblachery	Yanbian

Dairy & Beef

Domestication of the ancient Aurochs has
benefitted humans in many ways, and led
to many good things, namely ice cream, cheddar
cheese, milk shakes, sour cream, ribeye steaks, yogurt,
milk, cream cheese, filet mignon, butter, hamburger,
and (it deserves to be mentioned again) ice cream! This kind of
list makes the cow a unique and extremely valuable animal.

DAIRY

In the United States today, millions of cows produce billions of gallons of milk that are used for beverage milk products and for manufactured milk products such as ice cream, sour cream, yogurt, and cheese. In 2003, 9.08 million cows produced 170.3 billion pounds (19.8 billion gallons) of milk. On average, each cow produced 18,750 pounds (2,180 gallons) of milk. The total value of farm milk production in 2003 was $21.4 billion dollars.

Milk and dairy products are among the most highly regulated and monitored food products in the United States. Milk and dairy foods are subject to seventeen safety, quality, and sanitation inspections before reaching retail outlets.

Under the federal dairy program, there are four "classes" of milk. Class I describes milk used for fluid, or beverage, milk products. Class II refers to milk going into "soft" manufactured products such as sour cream, cottage cheese, ice cream, and yogurt. Class III refers to milk used for making hard cheeses, and Class IV is used to make butter and dry products such as non-fat dry milk.

In 2003, the U.S. milk supply was used to make the following products:

- 32.2% Fluid Milk
- 37.9% Cheese
- 12.9% Butter
- 8.6% Frozen Dairy products
- 1.0% Evaporated and Condensed Milk
- 0.7% used on the farms where it was produced
- 6.7% Other Uses

The dedication it takes to bring half-and-half to your local restaurant.

© Leigh Rubin

MILK

While it might seem that deriving milk from a cow is a pretty straight-forward task, what used to be performed by a milkmaid with a bucket is now much more complicated. High-tech automated milking machines make Holsteins look like

they're on the assembly line as record amounts of milk are yielded from today's dairy cows. Milk and dairy products are among the most strictly regulated foods because they are so perishable. The Food and Drug Administration (FDA) regulates dairy processing and enforces processing regulations.

Milk is collected from several farms and transported to a milk plant in large, refrigerated milk trucks. The mixing of milk allows the plant to produce a uniform product. Each farm's

milk differs in composition due to differences in breeds, genetics, feeding programs and temperature.

Fluid milk processing starts with standardization, an adjustment of the milk fat percentage to meet state and plant standards. Plants add skim milk to reduce fat percentages that are too high, and they add cream to increase milk fat percentages that are too low. While states have different standards, whole milk is 3.25 percent fat in most states.

3.25% milk fat

2% milk fat

less than 0.5% milk fat

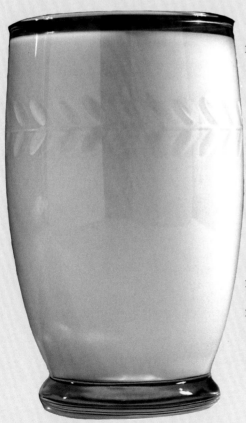

Plants also separate the fat particles from the liquid to produce low fat and skim milk. Lowfat milk contains 0.5 percent to 2.0 percent milk fat, while skim milk must have less than 0.5 percent milk fat. Lowfat and skim milk have become more popular drinks in recent years, as consumers have reduced the amount of fat in their diets.

Developed by Louis Pasteur in the mid-1800s, *pasteurization* is a very important part of milk processing. This step destroys any disease-causing bacteria by heating the milk. Most dairies heat milk to 161°F (71.5°C) for 15 seconds. This is called high-temperature, short-time pasteurization. Pasteurized milk can be kept for ten to 14 days under refrigeration.

Ultra-high temperature (UHT) pasteurization completely sterilizes the milk. This process heats milk to 280° (138°C) for two seconds. UHT processed milk can be stored at room temperature for at least three months without spoiling.

Pasteurized and UHT milk are immediately cooled to 45°F after heating. Then the milk is *homogenized*. If you take milk straight from a cow and allow it to sit in the refrigerator, it will separate into skim milk and cream. Homogenization uses pressure to squeeze milk through tiny valves, breaking up the fat globules to such a small size that they remain suspended evenly in the milk. Homogenized milk tastes richer and is easier to digest.

Pasteurized milk is fortified with vitamin D, and lowfat and skim milk are also fortified with vitamin A. Then milk is packaged in plastic jugs, paper cartons, or plastic bags, and distributed to retail markets.

BUTTER

It takes approximately twenty-one pounds of whole milk (a little more than two gallons) to make one pound of butter. Butter is basically the fat of the milk that when agitated (churned) coalesces and forms a solid. Homemade butter uses the cream directly from whole milk, while commercial butter is made by extracting small amounts of cream from whey, a by-product of cheese-making.

Once the cream is separated from the milk, it is held at cool temperatures to crystallize the butterfat globules to ensure proper churning and texture. From this "aging" tank, the cream is moved to a continuous churn where it is agitated. Agitation produces a semi-solid mass of butter, and buttermilk, the left-over liquid that is drained off and used elsewhere (people used to drink it, but today it is mainly used for baking). Salt is added to the butter to improve the flavor and shelf-life, and the butter is then worked to improve its consistency and flavor. Finally, the butter is patted into shape, wrapped in wax paper, and stored in a cool place where the butterfat crystallizes and the butter becomes firm.

Almost everything tastes better with butter!

An old-fashioned butter churn

Ice cream is made by mixing cream, milk, sugar, and flavorings (vanilla, chocolate, strawberry, etc.) and then carefully lowering the mixture's temperature until it sets. The discovery of using salt to control the mixture's temperature of the ingredients, along with the invention of the wooden bucket freezer with rotary paddles (above), were major breakthroughs in the creation of ice cream as we know it today. The first ice cream parlor in this country opened in New York City in 1776, and in 1851, Jacob Fussell in Baltimore established the first large-scale commercial ice cream plant that distributed ice cream to stores.

ICE CREAM

Over ninety percent of American households purchase ice cream, with the average American eating about forty-five pints (over five gallons) of ice cream a year! Over 1.6 billion gallons of ice cream are produced each year, with a market value of more than $20 billion dollars. Vanilla is the most popular flavor, with chocolate coming in a distant second.

The basic ingredients in ice cream are milk, cream, sugar, and flavorings, but stabilizers and sometimes egg yolks are added to keep the ice cream firm. Ice cream must contain at least twenty percent milk solids, of which at least ten percent must be milk fat. The cream used in making ice cream can be half-and-half (a mixture of milk and cream containing between 10.5 percent and 18 percent milk fat), light cream (between 18 percent and 30 percent milk fat), light whipping cream (between 30 percent and 36 percent milk fat), and heavy whipping cream (more than 36 percent milk fat).

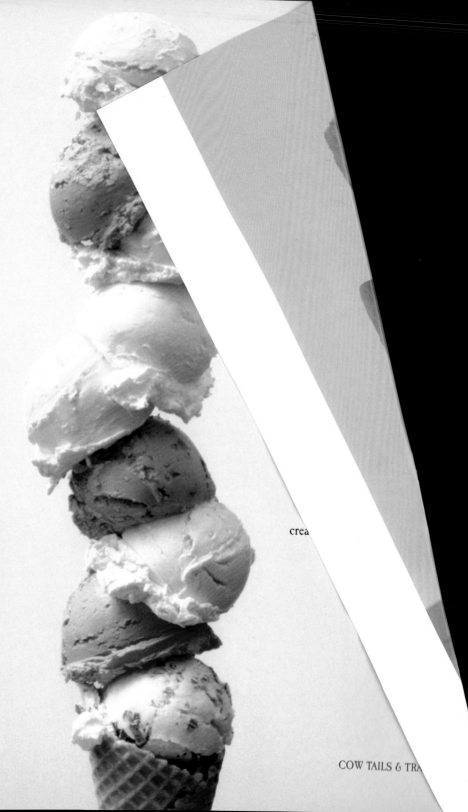

Until 1800, ice cream was a rare and exotic dessert enjoyed mostly by the elite. During the summer of 1790, President George Washington spent approximately $200 for ice cream. President Thomas Jefferson had a favorite 18-step recipe for an ice cream delicacy that resembled a modern-day Baked Alaska. In 1812, Dolly Madison served a magnificent strawberry ice cream creation at President Madison's second inaugural banquet at the White House. And in 1984, President Ronald Reagan declared July as National Ice Cream Month, and declared that patriotic Americans should mark the month with "appropriate ceremonies and activities."

crea

CHEESE

Americans love cheese, consuming thirty-one pounds per capita each year. A total of 8.6 billion pounds of cheese is made in America each year, most of which is produced in Wisconsin and California. According to the USDA Dairy Products Annual summary for 2003, five U.S. states together produced seventy percent of all cheeses made that year. They are: Wisconsin (25 percent); California (21 percent); New York (8 percent); Idaho (8 percent); Minnesota (7 percent).

While Americans love cheese, we are well behind the world's top cheese-consuming nations. Greece leads at fifty-six pounds consumed per person per year, followed by France (fifty-four pounds), Italy (fifty pounds), Denmark (forty-seven pounds), and Germany (forty-five pounds).

Basic Steps for Making Cheese

Every cheese is made in a different way, but these are the basic steps for making Cheddar cheese.

1) Bacteria is added to sterile, raw milk and left to ripen for about 18 hours.

2) The coagulated milk separates into curds and whey (solids and liquids). The curds are cut into sugar-cube-sized curds.

3) The curd is then heated so that it releases trapped whey. Once the desired acidity level is reached, the whey is drained off and the curd is stirred to prevent it from sticking together.

4) The curd is channeled to a draining table. The fragile curds need to be treated carefully to avoid losing precious fat or protein into the whey. (Whey is used to make whey cheeses such as Ricotta.)

5) The rest of the whey is gently squeezed out until the curd settles into a coherent mass on the draining table.

6) The mass of curds is cut into brick-sized blocks that are turned and piled on top of each other to force out more whey.

7) Gradually the bricks flatten as more whey is forced out. The acidity is checked constantly to make sure it is rising. The curd is ready for the next step only when it is coherent, dry, and firm.

8) The thin bricks are then milled to finger-sized pieces and mixed using giant forks to aerate and cool the curd while salt is added.

9) The dry curds are scooped into large, perforated, stainless steel molds lined with cheese cloth that are then placed in a press. Even pressure is gradually applied over 12 to 16 hours, forcing out any residual whey.

10) The following day, each cheese is turned out of its mold and unwrapped, then re-wrapped and replaced in the mold to be pressed again with increased pressure for another day.

11) The cheeses are unmolded and re-wrapped and sealed in fresh cloths. Labeled with the date, the cheeses are placed in a temperature-controlled environment to mature.

12) During the first few months, the Cheddars are regularly turned to move the moisture evenly through the curd. The natural molds on the cloth form a barrier against unwanted bacteria and allow the cheeses to mature until the cheesemaker decides they have reached their peak.

"Why do you always have to drag me along to the opera? *I* don't *need* to be cultured ... *You're* the one who makes the yogurt."

OTHER GOOD STUFF

YOGURT is milk fermented by Streptococcus thermophiles and either Lactobacillus acidophilus or Lactobacillus bulgaricus. Any sort of milk may be used to make yogurt, but most American-made yogurt is made with cow's milk. It is the fermentation of milk sugar (lactose) into lactic acid that gives yogurt its texture and tang. Fruit was first added to commercially-produced yogurt in 1946 by Dannon Yogurt. Americans eat over 300,000 tons of yogurt each year.

COTTAGE CHEESE is the fresh, drained curds of slightly-soured, low-fat, pasteurized milk. If the curds are allowed to drain longer, it is called pot cheese, and if the remaining moisture is pressed out so it becomes drier and crumbly, it is called farmer's cheese.

SHERBET is a frozen dessert made from iced sweetened fruit juice and low-fat milk. In the U.S. sherbet must have a milk-fat content between one and two percent; it must be sold as ice cream if the milkfat content is higher, or as sorbet if no milk is present at all.

GELATO is a dessert made from slowly frozen milk and water.

SOUR CREAM is cream that has been fermented by the bacteria Streptococcus lactis and Leuconostoc citrovorum.

CULTURED BUTTERMILK is fermented concentrated milk (water removed) using the same bacteria as sour cream.

CONDENSED MILK is milk that has been concentrated by evaporation, often with sugar added for longer shelf life. A patent for condensing milk was issued for Gail Borden in 1856.

EVAPORATED MILK is less concentrated than condensed milk, and has no sugar added. Sterilization is used to extend its shelf life.

CREAM CHEESE is produced by adding cream to milk, which is then curdled to form a rich curd. It is different than other cheeses in that it is not allowed time to mature and is meant to be consumed fresh. It was inspired by the French cheese Neufchatel.

MALTED MILK is malted barley and wheat flour mixed with whole milk that is then evaporated into a powder. It was created in the late 19th century by James and William Horlick as an easy-to-digest, high protein baby formula that they originally called Diastoid. It is also the basis for malted milkshakes that became popular in the 20th century.

The MILKSHAKE made it into the mainstream in 1922 when a Walgreens employee in Chicago took an old-fashioned malted milk (milk, chocolate, and malt) and added two scoops of ice cream.

The inventor of the BANANA SPLIT is debated, but Walgreen's is credited with spreading its popularity. Charles Walgreen adopted the banana split as the signature dessert in his chain of drugstores. Dairy Queen alone sells about 25 million banana splits each year.

Chocolate Chip vs. Oreo®

Unofficially, most Americans prefer milk and chocolate chip cookies two-to-one over milk and Oreo® cookies.

BEEF

Beef is the number one protein consumed in America and the demand continues to grow. Americans consume about 27 billion pounds of beef each year, which has a retail equivalent of $79 billion dollars. Between 33 and 36 million head of cattle are slaughtered each year, and from a 1,000 pound steer, approximately 432 pounds of retail beef is produced.

Beef is a valuable source of protein, niacin, vitamin B6 and B12, iron, phosphorus, and zinc. Fat, saturated fat, and cholesterol are also present in all meat; the amount varies depending on the species, the cut of meat, and the amount of marbling (fat) that is distributed within the lean.

Most of the beef consumed today comes from relatively young animals that are between two and three years old. The animal is most likely a steer (a castrated bull) or a "fed heifer," a cow that is raised for meat.

Before WWII, all American beef was "grass-finished," meaning that cattle ate pasture grass for the duration of their lives. Today, almost all beef cattle spend anywhere from 60 to 120 days

in feedlots being fattened with grain before being slaughtered. Corn finishing creates a well-marbled, fatty meat with a smooth, consistent flavor.

The U.S. federal government has been grading meat since 1926. The USDA meat grades are based on nationally-uniform standards of quality. Marbling, or streaks of fat through the meat, helps determine carcass grade; in general, the more marbling a cut of beef has, the more tender and flavorful it will be.

There are eight grades of meat: prime, choice, select, standard, commercial, utility, cutter, and canner. Generally, only three to five percent of the meat from one head of cattle is considered prime, and prime cuts of meat are not typically available in grocery stores but are used primarily in hotels and restaurants. The grade most widely sold at retail markets is choice, followed by select. Standard and commercial grades are "ungraded," meaning that supermarkets can stamp them with their own label. Utility, cutter, and canner grades are used for ground beef and hot dogs. Retired dairy or breeding cows are generally slaughtered between six and eight years of age, and their less tender meat is usually sold ungraded, as ground or otherwise processed.

Prizewinning beef at the fair

© Leigh Rubin

WHERE THE MEAT COMES FROM

1. CHUCK
Chuck Arm Pot Roast
Chuck Shoulder Pot Roast or Steak
Chuck Blade Steak
Chuck Short Ribs
Ground Beef

2. RIB
Rib Roast
Rib Steak
Ribeye Roast or Steak
Back Ribs

3. SHORT LOIN
Top Loin Steak
T-Bone Steak
Porterhouse Steak
Tenderloin Roast
Tenderloin Steak

4. SIRLOIN
Top Sirloin Steak
Bone Sirloin Steak
Boneless Sirloin Steak
Tri-Tip Roast
Tri-Tip Steak

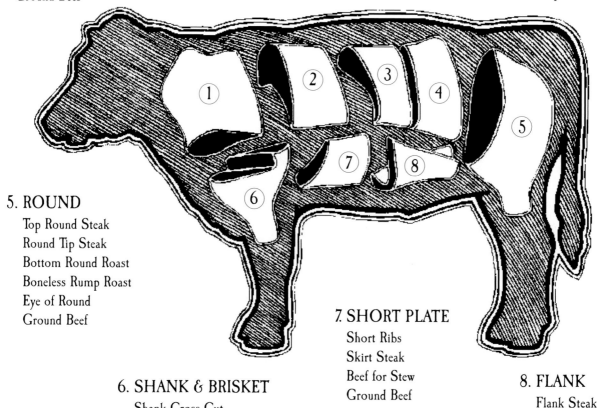

5. ROUND
Top Round Steak
Round Tip Steak
Bottom Round Roast
Boneless Rump Roast
Eye of Round
Ground Beef

7. SHORT PLATE
Short Ribs
Skirt Steak
Beef for Stew
Ground Beef

6. SHANK & BRISKET
Shank Cross Cut
Beef for Stew
Brisket

8. FLANK
Flank Steak
Ground Beef

HAMBURGERS

The hamburger is the most popular sandwich in America and is also the most popular way Americans consume beef. Americans eat approximately 29 billion hamburgers per year, an average of 120 per capita.

The invention of the hamburger—a cooked ground beef patty between two pieces of bread—is disputed, but it is named after the town of Hamburg, Germany, where a popular ground-beef steak was often served. Originally a ground beef patty was known as a "Hamburger steak" (first mentioned in an American cookbook in 1891), and when this was put between bread or in a bun it was called a "Hamburger sandwich." By the mid-20th century both terms were commonly shortened to "hamburger" or simply "burger."

The hamburger gained widespread recognition at the 1904 St. Louis World's Fair, and by the time Ray Kroc opened the first McDonald's franchise in the 1950s, the hamburger was already popular nationwide at diners and roadside stands. Today, McDonald's is the nation's largest purchaser of beef and potatoes, and every day about one quarter of the U.S. population eats fast food.

"Well, isn't life just full of surprises? ... You think you're gonna get pearly gates but end up with golden arches."

© Leigh Rubin

OTHER STUFF

If you take a 1,000-pound steer and obtain 432 pounds of retail beef, that leaves 568 pounds of "other stuff" that humans have used for as long as cattle have been used for food. Cattle provide us with many by-products—parts of the cow other than beef—that are used to create industrial, household, health, and food products. The following are some examples of how much we obtain and use from the cow.

Gelatin comes from the connective tissue of cattle and is used to make candy, dairy products, desserts, jellies, and marshmallows, while instrument strings, surgical sutures, and tennis racquet strings are all made from the intestines.

Numerous household products are derived from cattle by-products, including candles, ceramics, crayons, deodorants, cosmetics, insecticides, insulation, linoleum, perfume, mouthwash, photographic film, shaving cream, soaps, toothpaste, paint, and detergents. Antifreeze contains glycerol and asphalt contains

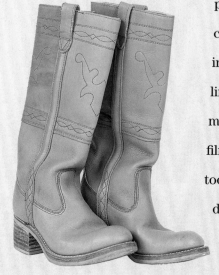

a binding agent that are both derived from beef fat. Beef fat is also used to make auto and jet lubricants, outboard engine oil, high performance greases, and brake fluid. Piano keys, cellophane wrap, bandage strips, emery boards, and collagen and bone for plastic surgery all come from the bones, horns, and hooves of cattle.

Leather made from the hides of cattle is widely used for clothing, sports equipment, saddles, luggage, footwear, and upholstery. It takes about 3,000 cowhides to produce the footballs for one season of the National Football League, and eleven basketballs can be made from one cowhide.